Passive Income

Ideas

Table of Contents

American Bar Association and should be considered as legally binding within the United States.

The reproduction, transmission, and duplication of any of the content found herein, including any specific or extended information will be done as an illegal act regardless of the end form the information ultimately takes. This includes copied versions of the work both physical, digital and audio unless express consent of the Publisher is provided beforehand. Any additional rights reserved.

Furthermore, the information that can be found within the pages described forthwith shall be considered both accurate and truthful when it comes to the recounting of facts. As such, any use, correct or incorrect, of the provided information will render the Publisher free of responsibility as to the actions taken outside of their direct purview. Regardless, there are zero scenarios where the original author or the Publisher can be deemed liable in any fashion for any damages or hardships that may result from any of the information discussed herein.

Additionally, the information in the following pages is intended only for informational purposes and should thus be thought of as universal. As befitting its nature, it is presented without assurance regarding its prolonged validity or interim quality. Trademarks that are mentioned are done without written consent and can in no way be considered an endorsement from the trademark holder.

Introduction

Congratulations on downloading *Passive Income Ideas*, and thank you for doing so. Many life-transforming ideas and discoveries are often hidden in books, and today, you get to partake in some of the greatest wisdom of the 21st century. You will learn or re-learn diverse ways to earn the passive income you need to better your life. You will get to meet an unmet need, treat yourself to something you have desired for a long time, or save to invest. There is a myriad of reasons why you would need extra money, and you have chosen the right book to guide you through the process.

To that end, the following chapters will seek to help you gain a deeper understanding of passive income and the process of acquiring it. Once you have understood that in the first chapter, the author will swiftly move on to open your eyes to opportunities that lie ahead of you, and each of them is a viable idea that can be taken up to generate some passive income.

The great passive income ideas include selling stock photos, placing ads on your car, starting a pyramid scheme, renting out your space, and starting an online class. You will also see how you can increase the interest rate for your savings by shifting your money from a regular to a high-yield account. You could also grow your income by investing in a business that you will manage yourself or get someone else to manage it.

The above ideas are only a few of the great moneymaking ideas in this book. Read it and see for yourself just how much earning potential around you is yet to be explored. I wish you well as you go ahead and implement a few of the ideas you pick up.

Thanks for choosing this book amongst the wide array of books available, we made sure this book give you the most information about this topic! Enjoy!

Chapter 1: What Is Passive Income?

Passive income is the regular earnings you get from a source other than working for your employer. The IRS defines passive income as income that one gets without active participation, like stock dividends, rental income, and book royalties. In contrast to what people think, passive income involves some work; you do not just lay on a couch and get a check; it also requires work, just relatively less than what your regular job requires.

Most people depend on active income that they get for their everyday work, and usually, after some days, a paycheck arrives. The problem with this kind of earning is that when you stop active work, for one reason or another, and the paychecks cease, you will only be left relying on the money you will have saved during your time working. Sadly, due to the current economic times, we do not get to save much, and relying on one source of income has become too risky.

Passive income is ideal for covering financial obligations that your current income does not satisfactorily cover. Some people desire to put much more money into their savings account, and getting a source of passive income is one of the best ways to go about it. Others want to pay off their debts, buy something they have been dreaming of, pay for a class, contribute towards a course, and other activities that their current engagements cannot sufficiently support.

You must have heard it said that the way to remain afloat, especially during times of financial uncertainty is to have multiple sources of income. This is because when one source fails, the others will fill up the gap. Therefore, in the event you lose your primary job, you will have other income sources that you can lean on, and this way, neither you nor your loved ones will suffer much from the change.

In addition, if you desire to build wealth, a single income source would not be sufficient; you need multiple sources, each putting something to the basket. It is easier to fill a basket when drawing from multiple sources in comparison to one source that could dry up from time to time.

For many that have difficulties saving, and always find themselves using up the money they had set aside, saving would be made easier if you directed the money from your alternative income sources directly to your savings account. In this way, you will not have any physical contact with your money, and for the first time in a long time, you will proudly be one of the savers.

One fact I can assure you about passive income is that it brings freedom. As the income flow becomes larger, and your capital builds, you acquire financial freedom. Your reliance on your job goes down, and you no longer have to put up with unfair treatment or harassment at work because you are not entirely reliant on your job. Some bosses are very cruel and unfair, and the only reason they have any employees is that the workers need money to support their families. However, once an employee has secured a steady passive income source, he or she has the freedom to walk out of the abusive situation finally.

Kindly note that passive income does not have to be trickling in small amounts; some passive income sources produce enough returns for some households depend on them fully. However, this is not to say that you will start a blog, and in three months, it is bringing in $20k. The process of growing income takes growth and patience. Therefore, don't start selling ads and quit your job; there is a process to it.

Among the great benefits or advantages of having a passive income source is a fact that you will finally begin to do something, you are passionate about. When looking for a passive income idea, many people look within themselves to determine what they are passionate about. It would be unfortunate if you took up a passive income source that sickens you. Imagine coming home only to start another activity that sucks the very life out of you. How miserable would you be? Again, imagine coming home from work to do what makes you happy, how quickly will you forget your job woes? As you choose among the passive income ideas, always ensure that you take up something that makes you happy, not the popular things that people in your circle are taking up, even when their ideas have the potential to bring in more money than what you are passionate about. After all, life is about making yourself, and not others, happy.

Go ahead and think about ideas that could help you make some extra money. The only requirement is that these ideas should be the ones that make you happy so that you have fun and you are passionate as you do the activities in them. In the meantime, here are some suggestions of some ways people use to bring in passive income.

Chapter 2: Passive Income Ideas

Idea #1: Investing In Real Estate

The real estate investment option has two alternatives. You could choose to invest in real estate by directly purchasing and owning real estate property, or you could join others in mobilizing resources to be used by a direct investor to purchase or to develop real estate.

One of the ways to invest in real estate directly is by owning investment properties. By definition, an investment property is a property that you have purchased for the sole purpose of drawing revenue from it. Revenue is earned by either leasing the property or by reselling the property at a profit. These kinds of investment projects include the purchase of commercial rental property that businesses can lease to run their operations, or purchasing an apartment building collecting rental income from the tenants.

The advantage of owning rental property is that its value may increase even as you earn income from it, over the long-term. You also stand to gain tax benefits because the property is depreciating. However, owning an investment property requires a great deal of capital upfront and some significant capital for maintenance of the property. It also requires your hands-on attention because you will not solely depend on a manager to run things for you; as we mentioned earlier, passive income requires some bit of work. In line with that, also expect some large, costly, and unexpected liabilities, which you might not have anticipated at the beginning.

Note that if you decide to purchase an investment property and you needed to sell it to get some money; the property is relatively illiquid and would take a long time to sell, sometimes even months. Your property might also have depreciated significantly and lost value with time.

The second alternative, crowdfunding, also known as private equity funds. A private equity fund is an investment fund that brings together investors and pools their funds for real estate investment. These funds consist of different real estate investment types, and this increases the diversification of the investor's portfolio. The advantage of being a part of this is not only in the gains but also in the fact that this method is suitable for investors who have no real estate knowledge because the can rely on the expertise of the real estate managers in charge of these funds. The managers often employ diligence in their works to attract more investors, to grow the pool of funds.

The traditional set up of the private equity fund investment was quite illiquid and difficult to get into because of its high initial cost requirement. Only high net worth individuals and institutional investors could meet the entry requirements. However, crowdfunding, as it currently stands, is open to investors of all classes,

Another real estate investment alternative is Real Estate Investment Trusts (REITs). REITs offer a large portfolio of income-producing real estate investment properties. Ninety percent of the earnings from REITs should be distributed to the investors, by law, and so far, this investment channel has attracted over 70 million American investors.

Public REITs are of two types: the traded and the untraded. The publicly traded REITs offer the advantage of liquidity because they are openly traded at the stock exchange. The liquidity is then priced into the cost of the shares, which results into a 'liquidity premium' that new investors are required to pay to be able to purchase and sell the asset they have in mind.

Sadly, this liquidity premium leads to lesser returns on the side of the investors, regardless of whether they are selling their shares or not. In addition, the REITs market is said to move in congruence with the rest of the investment market, thereby moving just like the stock market, even when nothing has happened in regards to the underlying property.

Non-traded REITs are slowly becoming more popular because the dividends have maintained a double-digit figure, but the downside is that they charge very high upfront fees to new investors, and there is no disclosure regarding the source of these fees.

Mistakes to Avoid In Passive Real Estate Income Generation

- Lack of steady adequate cash flow: In your real estate ownership, the primary goal is to have a steady cash flow, and to have your property appreciate. However, changes in the market could bring hurdles to your dream. However, this is bad because you need some cash flow to be able to maintain your property. This maintenance safeguards your rental income.

- Not being ready to become a landlord: A landlord should know how to create the ideal living environment by coming up with rules and holding tenants accountable for keeping them, from the first day they step into your property. Some tenants tend to take advantage of the landlord's kindness and will fall into negative patterns like paying their rents late. Know that these behaviors will hurt your cash flow.

- Failing to screen the tenants thoroughly: One of the ways to ensure a steady income flow is by ensuring that you only lease to faithful, responsible tenants. Take time to screen potential clients to keep yourself from things that could hurt your income like possible lawsuits, expensive eviction practices, and property damage.

- Failure to be part of the active management: While you could leave your property in the hands of an able property management body, the best way to go about the management is to be active in it. See to it that your manager is providing the best living environment to your tenants, without harassing them. Ensure that care and management are done properly to ensure that the value of your property is not going down.

Idea #2: Having a High-Yield Savings Account

The way to get a passive income stream flowing when you have less money is to save it in a high-yielding savings account. This could be a certificate of deposit account, or a money market account, but this all depends on your financial goals.

Money Market and CD Accounts

A money market account is just like your traditional savings account only that its interest rates are higher and you will need to have a higher running balance. This account is different from the typical savings account mainly because the banks can use it to invest in notes, treasury, and bonds, besides loaning it out to borrowers. There are far fewer restrictions on what the banks can do with your money. Almost all banks, both online and brick-and-mortar, have these accounts. You can also access them through a broker account, such as those that fund your 401 and Roth IRA. Confirm that your brokerage offers these accounts, and see what the interest rate charged is.

A Certificate of Deposit (CD) account is just like your typical savings account, but for the customer accepted to keep the money in the said account for a particular term. For your commitment, the bank, in turn, offers you a high-interest rate.

Both the money market and the CD account are short-term savings accounts, but with a CD account, the interest rate remains constant for as long as you are holding your account. The interest rate varies, however, when it comes to the money market account.

Another difference with these accounts is that the money market account typically demands a large initial deposit than CD accounts demands. It is also true that you cannot withdraw money from a CD account via an ATM or write checks, but a money market account allows it.

Since the interest rate, and other terms of a CD account are fixed, you must leave your money in your account until the agreed upon term is done. If you choose to withdraw your money earlier, you will be asked to pay the penalty. On the other hand, money market accounts are quite flexible and do not attract any penalties. However, account holders can only withdraw money in a limited number of times (6 withdrawals per month).

As you can see, either of these options offers an interesting and attractive deal, but if you want to grow your income without being tempted to withdraw the money when the need arises, choose a CD account; you will be glad you waited.

Online Savings Account

To have an online savings account, all you have to do is move your money from your current savings account that has low interest, to your high-yielding online bank account. This move will yield some extra cash. Do not be worried that everything is done virtually because online banks have FDIC insurance, just like your traditional brick-and-mortar bank.

Realize that if you have all your cash stacked in a traditional savings account, you are leaving money on the table, and cumulatively, this money you could use to finance a vacation, a spa day, or an investment that will also give you some additional passive income.

Besides the higher interest rates, an online account has other advantages, including the absence of fees, lower minimum requirements, and the fact that it is convenient, so customers can access it from any location.

Unfortunately, this account will hold your money for longer periods and does not offer any face-to-face interaction that some customers prefer having.

Take note that the process of linking your new online account to your old one could well take a few extra days.

Idea #3: Rent Out Your Space

There recently has risen the 'sharing culture' or the 'sharing economy,' born of the practice of people renting out their stuff or their spaces when they do not need to use them. Many ideas have grown from this new development, and people have no issue sharing their spare rooms, houses, cars, driveways, garden, storage space, office space, and other things.

House or a Spare Room

Courtesy of Airbnb, you could rent out your spare room, or even your entire house when you go away on a trip. The good thing about this arrangement is that you get to set your own prices, whether you are charging on a per-month or a per-night basis. You also get to choose whether to rent out your living space for the short-term or for the long-term depending on your schedule and preference. Do not be worried about safety issues because the Host Guarantee reimburses all eligible hosts with up to a million dollars in damages.

You also will not need to pay a fee to get on the Airbnb platform; the only costs you will bear are those of maintenance and cleaning. Seeing that you have nothing to lose, you should consider trying it.

Car or Car Parking Space

The practice of renting out your car has been in existence for a while now. However, did you know that you could also make money from renting out that parking space that is not in use? The SpotHero app will help to facilitate this, for people living in New York. You only need to list your parking space on the app, set your rates, and indicate when space will be available. People interested in using your spot will contact you via message, and if space is available, you will allow them to park their cars in it for the time for which they paid.

If your parking space is available all year round, you get to earn an income throughout the year. Do not be worried about your payments or the contacts of your customers because the app managers will do that for you. Your payments reflect in your bank account after some time.

Your Stuff

Did you know that you could rent anything in your home that you are not using? You can rent your tools and other items to neighbors, and even strangers. There are already apps that will connect you to people who need to rent out stuff from you for a short time, and some will even offer to buy it.

The hoarding culture has slowly crept to consumers across the world, and people now have a tendency to purchasing items they do not necessarily need. Looking around your living room, the garage, or the storage unit, you may uncover lots of items that you do not normally use, and with luck, you could make some money off of it. This equipment could include camera equipment, drones, sports equipment, power tools, game consoles, musical instruments, gardening tools, speakers, and others.

Garden

Unbelievably, you could have someone else use your garden, at a cost. They do not have to be farming, they might even be camping in tents outside your home. If you would not be comfortable having people renting out your extra space in the house, the outside is also good enough. You may have to let them use your toilet, but if this is something you hope to do in the long-term, you could construct decent washrooms at the edge of your garden.

People with big neat gardens will also hire them out for sports, weddings, and summer barbeques.

Storage Space

If you have recently cleared your storage unit, you may have a bit of space that someone else may need. You do not have to own a storage container; there could be space in your basement, attic, garage, loft and cupboards. Thanks to the high rent payments for a storage container, people are now open to storing their property in other people's homes, and there are apps to facilitate that. For your idle space, you could easily earn a few dollars per week, and this could translate to thousands of dollars of unexpected income per year.

Once you have a steady customer, you do not have to keep checking your email for new bookings. You only have to receive your guaranteed weekly payments.

Home Office

If you mind having a new person with you in the house at night, why not have they come over during the day when you are not around? If your desk at home is not in use during the day, on working hours, and you have a stable internet connection, why not rent out your home office to a freelancer or a person starting out a new company who needs cheap working space? This option is popular in large cities, and it could earn you a decent daily income.

Other people would want your space for a quick nap, a space to conduct their psychology or physiotherapy sessions, or as a good setting for a movie or an advert. Imagine having your home in some fancy advert, showcasing your décor prowess! Never mind about the perverts that may want to use your space for weird reasons.

You can control what your space is used for by asking the tenants some upfront questions, and popping in uninvited to verify that they are using your space for what it was rented for.

For all these ideas, you remain the boss.

Idea #4: Come Up With an Online Class or Course

You obviously have learned something in your craft that other people have not. Our experiences are often unique, and if you think that yours have caused you to have some special knowledge, it would only be right if you taught and mentored others, at a fee. This is what has caused the online learning industry to be worth quite an amount of money. It is one way for you to get yourself some passive income.

The amount you make from your online classes is proportionate to the amount of time and effort that you put into marketing your classes, and the quality you deliver to your students. It also helps if you can pitch your course to the right audience, at the right time, and in a helpful manner.

Here's how to go about it: select a topic or subject that you are very good at, and explore it even deeper. Do it much more than a podcast or a blog post would do. Ensure that you gain an in-depth understanding of the topic.

You need to identify the teaching method you will be using to reach your students. Will you deliver the material via videos, or will you use text? Will you include practice exercises? Look into all these details. Don't forget how important it is to market your course as we have mentioned above.

Once your class is up and running, ensure that you foster a sense of community in your class. Have your learners form slack communities, WhatsApp groups, and Facebook groups. Also, ensure that you keep them engaged with some homework.

If you are sure that you will be able to deliver a quality learning experience, begin to charge a premium price for your services.

Idea #5: Have a Side Business

A side business can be a good source of passive income, but the key to succeeding in it is having the right people running it for you. You may own the business by starting one from scratch or buying an existing one. You could also become a part owner in an existing business, and leave the management to the original entrepreneur.

Buying an Existing Business

You can buy an existing business, one that is flourishing, and profit from the existing setup with only little effort. If you retain the management and the staff, you only have to do very little because they already understand how the system works. For example, you could buy a restaurant or even a blog. In the case of the restaurant, you will already have a staff and a market, and in the case of a blog, you will already have committed readers, which eliminates the need to market the business vigorously, as you would do with a new business.

If you have the chance to buy a monetized popular website that has affiliates, even if you do not add any piece of content to it, and you leave it as is, expect to make some passive income from it.

It is possible also to buy a struggling business, and this is great if you already know how to operate a business like it because then, you will know the improvements that are needed. For example, if it is a restaurant, and you establish that the issue lies in the quality of food and the service, you will go ahead and change the suppliers, and either re-train the service staff or hire new staff. The business will be in your hands, and you can go ahead and make all the changes you believe are needed to turn around the profits from it.

Buying Ownership in an Existing Business

You could also become a silent partner by identifying a good business that needs capital for expansion. Rather than offering your money on loan, opt to have equity in the business. The business owner will continue running the operations of the business while you, as the silent partner, only get to share in the profits.

This form of ownership is ideal because that is how many wealthy people have built their wealth. Look at the business moguls at 'Shark Tank,' they are always seeking a share in a business they perceive to be profitable in the future. This way, they get the entrepreneurs to work and grow their money, for as long as the business exists. The secret to succeeding in this endeavor is to only choose to invest in businesses that have a future.

In addition, investing in multiple businesses like this is safe because you get to spread your risk, rather than burying all your capital in a start-up of your own, whose future is uncertain. With a diversified portfolio, you will not be left shaken whenever there are changes in the market.

Outsourcing a Business

Once you have a business going, either because you have started it or bought it, and are not willing or able to manage it yourself, you can outsource it. Outsourcing refers to getting skilled professionals to manage affairs on your behalf so that you can have time to focus on other equally important tasks. This way, there is more income from all your activities, and no side will suffer from poor management.

For example, rather than hiring employees to work in your editing firm, you could hire freelancers to work as contract laborers. The freelancers should have a strong work ethic and be skilled enough to produce good results.

Some of the companies that will link you with the freelancers you are looking for include Upwork, CloudPeeps, Guru, Fiverr, and PeoplePerHour.

Bottom line, whether you choose to buy an existing business, start your own, or outsource, starting a side business is a great way to ensure an inflow of passive income.

Idea #6: Photo Licensing

Digital photography has opened up a world where more and more people are using their cameras to document various moments of their lives. The photos are taken using tablets, smartphones, and regular cameras. Taking these pictures tends to be quite fun, but without knowing it, people have stocked lots of pictures that could be earning them some dollars, through licensing.

Making money out of photography is the best example of how a person can turn a hobby into a source of passive income. All it will take is for you to gain a better understanding of what the sites to which you should post are looking for, and what you need to do to reach those standards. Another perk in the whole deal is that you get to do all this at your own time, from the comfort of your home.

The first thing you could do to know what clients are looking for is to look at the pictures that these potential clients usually use. Look at the images in their products, brochures, websites, and ads. In most cases, none of the photos were taken by a professional photographer in the traditional way. Most were probably taken by amateur and semi-professional photographers, then licensed as stock photos (a stock photo is a photo that is used for multiple purposes).

The way this works is that the artist will take the stock photo, of a model, a beautiful scenery in the wild, a sunset or any other beautiful site and he or she will then upload that photo to a stock photo site that will be the broker that comes between the artist and the potential clients. It is likely that more than one client will take an interest in the photo, meaning that the photo will be used many times, ten or even a thousand times. The more the photo is used, the more the money collected from the clients.

Every time a client licenses an image, you and the stock photo house will receive some money, depending on the prices and fees you negotiated at the beginning. You will stand to make some good income taking this method.

That is how the money factors come into play in photo licensing.

Imagine if you took a number of good photos such that you have quite a nice selection from which the clients can choose, you then stand to gain a lot of returns. One morning, you will wake up to find $10 in your account, sometimes $100 and it can even get to the thousands. The possibilities are endless.

So, how do you venture into this money-making venture? It is quite simple. You first need to have a collection of quality photos that you feel someone would want to see it. If you are having doubts about some quirky photo, so long as it is of good quality, put it into the collection because someone could have a good use for it. Ensure that you do not include any photo that is not well done, or out of focus because even before it gets to the client, the stock house will reject it.

The next step to take is to approach one of the reputable stock photo brokers in the market. Consider Shutterstock.com, iStockphotos.com, or Freedigitalphotos.net, among others. These sites will offer some instructions upfront, on the kind of photos they need. They will even give you some important tips about how you can take better photos, in addition to offering you answers to some technical questions.

Since you have the luxury of choosing from among different stock photo houses, take your time and read their terms, and also check to see their payout rates. In your sign up, ensure that you do not offer to be an exclusive contributor unless you are sure that you will only be working with this specific site. Most photographers find it better to sign up with several sites, as a way to diversify their 'portfolio' and to take advantage of different terms offered.

Do not be too quick to give up your photos though; you need to be aware of some facts. The first is the reality that not all photos will be good enough for the stock photo house. These houses only source for the best of the best. They want to please their clients and ensure that they have secured their business. Therefore, your images should be of the highest quality and should cover an aspect that will somewhat be useful to the potential client (clients will be looking for photos that match a particular theme, those that communicate a message). Clients will not pick a photo just because it is beautiful.

Secondly, you should realize that you will immediately lose control of your images. Suppose you are a man with a beautiful daughter or wife, once you submit the picture and the client chooses it, nothing you would do to stop the client from using your picture for his or her advertising campaign against child molestation, domestic abuse or for breast cancer awareness. How bad and utterly embarrassing would it be if your child or wife was used for a cause like that one?

Therefore, even if you take great pictures of your family, ensure that you only upload generic pictures, the kind that would not concern you even if it was used for whichever cause.

The third aspect to take caution about is the fact that you ought to pay close attention to the details of the copyright agreement you are signing. The terms of your contract will vary from one stock photo house to the other. Ensure that you go over the entire contract, paying attention to the fine print and that you understand the rights that you have in regards to the photos, as an artist. Ensure that you do not put yourself in a situation where it is illegal for you to use your own photos just because you submitted them to a platform.

All legalities should be well understood before you commit to any.

Idea #7: Using Your Car for Ad Space

Here is where it gets interesting people! The business only requires you and your car. How simple! The taxi business, Uber and other transportation means have become very crowded, which has lessened the demand for transportation services. In addition, some people have issues allowing strangers into their cars. In either of the situations described above, the solution is car wrapping.

Many people are paid by car ad wrapping companies to advertise local and large businesses across town. An ad will be placed on the deck, on the hood, or other places, on your car, and your duty is to drive around in it so people in your locality can see the ad message. This business, however, is only for people who do not mind having stuff imprinted on their cars, because to them, a car is only a convenient tool that moves them from one point to the next. As a result, car wrapping has become one of the better-paying side hustles that require little, if any, effort.

Much to my shock, car wrapping has existed for a long time, although there is not much buzz about it. People have been getting fat checks for doing it, as big as $500 and more, every month. If you are constantly on the road, or you like to take a drive at least once in a day, car wrapping would be an ideal way for you to earn some decent money. You will be earning on your drive to school, to the store, to work, and to any other location you drive to, and the proceeds from this hustle could go to your savings account or your retirement account.

Before you go any further, realize that the ads on your car could range from a simple decal sticker placed on the side of your car, or the car could be completely covered, wrapped from the trunk to the hood, to catch the eye of the intended audience. It has been found that people are more attracted to moving than to stationary ads on billboards. As such, a driver will very likely read an ad on your car better than he or she will read a billboard ahead.

Commonly, the businesses advertising will be large Fortune 500 companies, but once in a while, you will also find small local businesses taking up this advertising media because they want to take advantage of the low-cost advertising. As the driver, you will be handed some vinyl stickers displaying the company logos and trademarks, and you will be required to place them on your car strategically. The more the ads you have on your car, the larger the surface covered, and typically, the money paid out to you will also be higher.

All persons who wish to participate in this hustle as car drivers have to undergo some form of vetting process to ensure that they meet the requirements of the advertising company. Come to think of it, if you take up the job but keep your car hidden in the garage all day, of what benefit will the ad on your car be to the business? Therefore, drivers must be prescreened to ensure that they fit the bill for their advertising gig.

You will be asked to state the make and model of your car, the year it was made, the route you normally take on a regular basis and the number of hours you spend on the road. These are the typical questions, but as you would expect, each car wrapping company will have its own set of questions based on its policies and requirements. Do not take the questions personally; they are only meant to ensure that once you get the job, the advertising message will be placed at a proper spot and that the marketing message will be spread out across the target area, to the target population.

As such, expect a minimum mileage requirement for every week, you may also be restricted to the things that you can put inside or on the car, like personal bumper stickers. If you are selected, you will be informed of the money to expect, and after how long. The money paid to you, as we have pointed out, will depend on the type of car you are driving, the route you take on a daily basis, the size of the ad, and the time you typically spend on the road. On average, you could receive somewhere between $400 and $500. However, the payout you receive largely depends on the company you are working for.

In general, here are the requirements you need to become a driver for a car wrapping company. You must be of legal age to drive a car, and have a clean driving record, at that. Your car must have a GPS system installed in it, either bought by you or installed by the advertisers. You must also ensure that for the contract period, the ads remain in place. Lastly, you must meet the minimum mileage requirement for each week or month.

49

Idea #8: Start Your Blog/Vlog

So, you love writing, and would like to reach a bigger audience, and earn some money while at it? Well, welcome to blogging. Blogging in recent times has quite a positive reputation. It is praised as a source of good passive income, and for a good reason. Some people have abandoned their 9 to 5 jobs and have focused all their effort to the blogs; they earn somewhere from $5,000 to $25,000 per month, and this is on the lower side. Others earn millions.

Don't let the numbers fool you into thinking that this is a get-rich-quick gig because it is not. The reality is that the process of getting any decent income from blogging is painfully slow, and will require a lot of your patience. However, you will be better off starting right now, so that you begin to grow your account now. Here's how:

The first and most critical step is to identify your niche. A niche allows you to come up with a plan on how to go about. There are only five major niches: health, happiness, love, wealth and hobbies that you are extremely passionate about like traveling. However, since there will be many writers creating content on these five broad categories, what will make you stand out in the market is getting more specific with your niche.

What will help you iron out the situation is coming up with a concrete plan. For this, you need to conduct research, making it as in-depth as possible. A great place to start it all is to examine your own interests. For example, if you enjoy sports, hiking, and other outdoor activities, opt to write about this, rather than on 'fun indoor activities' that you may only know little about. Your content will not compare with that of another blogger who spends more time indoors and has learned a few tricks to make the indoor as interesting as the outdoor activities.

Try to think outside the box too by brainstorming and coming up with ideas that others would not normally come up with. It is important that you make your writing as interesting as possible, but truthful so that your readers will be entertained and educated at the same time.

Next, how shall you get people interested in what you are writing? How shall you generate traffic to your blog? You only need to turn to Google Ads again, to see the number of persons that are searching for the stuff you intend to create. Turn to the 'Google Keyword Planner' and input the terms you will be using. For example, if you wish to write about healthy weight loss, one common term in your writing will be 'healthy weight loss' or any other similar statement; it doesn't have to be the exact heading. Google will add to your search other terms related to what you typed in.

If the number of people interested in the topic you have chosen is high, then we could say that your niche is profitable, has a growing audience, and that it is something you would want to center your blog around.

Besides Google, use social media sites to see what's buzzing, to see the niches that are making money, and to gauge whether these niches are growing, or shrinking. That in-depth investigation is good and will save you some headaches later in life.

Once the details are figured out, it is time to start the blot itself. The best money saver for making a professional blog is self-hosted WordPress. Most bloggers use it. However, new bloggers can try BlueHost because it only costs $2.95 each month for the first 36 months.

With your blog in place, you now should concentrate on creating great content for your readers. Kindly keep in mind that readers are only attracted to great, not good, content. Quality matters greatly because there are millions of blog posts produced across the world, and with people's limited attention span and loyalty, you need some attention-grabbing content that will keep your readers coming back. Your readers should be able to share your content with others on social media, and if they are bloggers too, they can recommend your work to their readers too.

Once you create content, pass it through a thorough review, where you measure to see whether your writing is in-depth, well formatted, has links to other posts that will expound on the points you have made, has relevant images, and on top of all that, it should be entertaining.

One key component of your blogging is the audience. Once you have a following, making money off your content becomes very easy.

Therefore, work on promoting your blog either through SEO writing, advertising on social media, and paid to advertise.

One secret buried deep in the blogging circles is the need to have an email list. An email list is a strategy for maintaining your regular readers, and a way to strengthen your personal brand. Most readers come once, then leave forever. However, when you are able to gather their email addresses through 'GetResponse' or 'Awebber.' Have something to offer your readers, like 7-day free access to a course if you are running an online course, or any other thing you feel would appeal to your audience. Seek to increase your reading list continually, beyond the current readers, month after month.

Vlogging

Vlogging is more or less similar to blogging, only that your communication media will be videos instead of typing words. In a world where we take videos to capture all kinds of moments, this should be easy.

There are four ways to earn money by making videos. The first is through paid or sponsored posts. Companies that are seeking to promote their brand order these videos. For this option, you and your video become influencers to a particular audience, in exchange for money or products, depending on the company, and the deal you entered into.

However, deals like these are only offered to vloggers with a large audience, or at least five to ten thousand. Your audience should also have an interest in what you are offering.

Overall, sponsored posts are the most coveted kind of blogs, because they have the highest returns, but the downside is that it is very difficult to achieve the publicity needed to land deals like these.

The second way to vlog is to sell merchandise. You can create a vlog as a platform to promote your crafts, from logos and designs to clothes and beauty products. Anything sellable can be promoted using blogs.

You could also vlog about a healthy diet you are taking, and in this vlog, you could introduce your cookbook or diet plan. You could also educate your viewers on some home-made products they could make. With vlogging, anything flies. If you need to advertise your eBooks and online tutorials, Sellfy offers the best platform.

The third way to make money vlogging is by putting up YouTube ads. To monetize your

YouTube channel, you are required to have at least 1000 subscribers, and to have accumulated 4,000 watch hours in the last 12 months. Only then, can you apply for the YouTube Partner Programme, and begin displaying ads in your videos.

When YouTube has checked and approved your channel, then you may begin to display ads, and when your viewers click on those ads, you will be paid.

Another way vlogging can earn you an income is via affiliate links. It is easier to land affiliate sponsorship compared to sponsored posts, but the income from them is lesser

To become an affiliate marketer, identify brands and products you wish to promote and get into their affiliate programs. Alternatively, when you get into the Amazon Associates program, you will have the platform to advertise and speak about the products you are already using. If your viewer makes a purchase, you will receive a payment.

Idea #9: Shopping

How would you like to earn money while conducting one of your favorite activities, shopping? Well, to be fair, not everyone enjoys shopping, possibly because of the effort and time it takes to find the right product. Negotiating with a seller can also make this process unbearable. That said, however, anyone feels about shopping; we all do it every now and then. How would you like to earn some passive money while shopping?

The idea of spending money to earn money seems counterproductive, but it is a cool way to generate passive income. You will find that many shopping sites and outlets around you offer their customers special rewards for shopping in their stores. Majority of these sites have partnered with online retailers. Therefore, whenever you want to buy something, you might as well opt to buy from these sites so that you can earn some special rewards and some cash back. One popular site that does this is Ebates. Through its websites, it offers cash back and some coupon codes, among other kinds of rewards.

Occasionally, there are also some double cash back specials, and they provide a great way to double the earnings you get from these websites.

Some credit cards also that give back some cash for your shopping, with the return rate ranging from 1% to 5% of the amount spent. Others offer reward points that you can redeem to get something or a service, just as you earn miles when you fly.

Be careful though, so that your quest to earn some cash back does not override rational money use. Stick to purchases that you intended to make, with or without the rewards.

Idea #10: Start a Pyramid Scheme

A pyramid scheme is a great way to take advantage of other people's efforts and money to make a killing, but only if you are at the top of the pyramid. Sounds crude, right? Yes, it is. It is chilling to think that people still fall for it since 1919 when Charles Ponzi came up with the idea of a pyramid scheme promising 50% interest for money lent, in only 90 days. Ponzi garnered 15 million dollars from his venture before he was arrested and sent to jail, before he was deported in 1934, back to Italy. While Ponzi may have been thrown out of the country, his genius idea did not die, and opportunists have used this scheme to earn from the sweat of gullible people.

The reason pyramid schemes seem to have nine lives is primarily because of how innocently they begin. First, they have been given quite a sweet name, and have been rebranded as Multi-Level

Marketing (MLM). Each MLM is centered on a product, but if you are careful to observe, the main focus is on the continuous recruitment of members. Their life depends on the recruitment of members, who are also somewhat convinced to purchase the products.

Almost everyone in an MLM loses money but for those at the top who earn a larger share, and a few other members who earn a little money. However, in the spirit of making some passive income, here's how to start your own pyramid scheme.

The first thing is to identify a service or a product that you can market as revolutionary. The product you come up with could be some tea that restores the skin and prevents aging, or some juice that restores the digestive system or some unusual financial opportunity designed to turn around your fortune immediately. The key to making the people buy into your idea is to make the service or product sound as convincing as possible. Make it sound like something the people have never heard about like it delivers results better than anything that existed before that one.

The second step requires you to come up with a commission structure that is not easily understood. It should assuredly pay the first 8 to 10 people at the top of the tier as soon as a purchase or other payment is made. This will be good because as the people at the top get large gains, the people at the bottom will be excited about the possibilities and will continue to invest, in the hope that they too will get to those levels.

Thirdly, you must be careful not to ever use the term 'multi-level marketing' or 'pyramid scheme' in your operations. Although they perfectly describe what you are doing, they have a negative connotation that could drive your customers away. Avoid them at all costs. Instead, take up terms like 'network marketing,' 'binary compensation' and 'dual marketing.' To make it even more convincing, you should come up with a brand-new name, so that your 'system' has no connection to any other MLM whose reputation could have been soiled. Always aim to appear different.

You wouldn't make your way into people's pockets if you didn't sound credible. Credibility in this setup is built through endorsements from people who look and sound important. Get prestigious business publications to write about you, get respected society members to support you.

Next, you need to attach a high price to your service or product. This step is important for two reasons, the first being that it ensures a steady high income for the members at the top tier, and the fact that a high price is associated with quality products.

The last thing you want is to have too many people receiving the returns willy-nilly. As such, there must be strict and almost impossible requirements for members to move up. For example, require the new members to have a particular minimum product purchase in addition to having a number of new recruits. This ensures that there is a constant flow into your business. It is likely that the new associates will bring in their family members so that they can begin their ascent. Throw these a few dollars to keep their efforts building.

From the onset, you should have some early adopters. These are the people who will be receiving some substantial gains and will be used as the 'success stories' of your project. They will be the demonstrations of how all financial dreams can come true for members after becoming part of your system.

Not forgetting, there should be 'tools' to keep members engaged and committed to the dream. People may begin to seem like they have wasted their money, but if you keep them engaged, they will always gravitate back to the cause. Training materials and tools do the magic here. They should be designed to reassure the members that someday in the future, they will become successful.

Besides the tools, ensure that your company is holding periodic events, in different places, to get people excited and to recommit themselves to your setup. Always ensure that your events parade the strategically chosen success stories so that others will be excited about joining your company.

Having done that, you can sit back and enjoy your massive passive income as it flows in. Keep the dream alive, ensure that your focus appears to be on helping people achieve the financial freedom you now enjoy. Dreamers will keep pouring their resources to you, and you will stand to benefit, every time.

Idea #11: Affiliate Marketing

Affiliate marketing is the process of generating traffic or sales for an online retailer through referrals, in exchange for some commission. It begins with you recommending a service or a product to people who follow you on various social platforms, and if they purchase the product or service, the advertising company will accord you a commission for all sales made following your affiliate link.

Becoming an affiliate marketer is not something that you just wake up and fall into, it takes proper planning, time and effort to become good at it.

The first thing to do is to establish your niche because identifying a specific area to work with will give you some focus and guide you in your content creation process. Making targeted marketing campaigns will not be difficult either. The way to identify your niche is to think about what you are passionate about.

Once you have identified the field for which you have a passion, go ahead and set up your blog or your website. Tell the people about who you are, indicate your contact information, let them know that your website is monetized, and indicate your terms of service. Ensure that you have a custom 404 page because it significantly improves the user's experience. Also, include a page for advertisers and indicate whether there are available slots for them to advertise, the size of your audience, their demographics and how the advertiser can contact you. Ensure that your policies are clear upfront, to avoid misunderstandings when you sign up to be a marketer.

When everything is done, go ahead and create content using products that you already use. It is from this content that advertisers will gauge your suitability to market their products. If it is good, get ready for some business.

Idea #12: Install Vending Machines

The idea of earning income from the installation of vending machines is not new at all. They have been everywhere for as long as many of us can remember. Despite being an old idea, though, this business has not ceased to be a lucrative business seeing that it generates billions of dollars annually.

Anyone can start the vending machine business, whether a new or an experienced entrepreneur. You only need an ideal location, to be connected to some low-cost product suppliers and access to a vending machine, either new or used.

For anyone looking for a lucrative side hustle that needs only a little capital to start, this would be the ideal way to expand and build your portfolio. You can start with as low as $2,000 capital, and if you choose your products right, install your vending machine at the proper place, and have a friendly user interface, your machine can earn you a consistent income of between $600 and $800 each month.

While everything else seems rosy, the process of starting the business is not as easy; you need to engage in some logistical and financial planning beforehand. Even before you get down to the nitty-gritty of the business such as sourcing machines and assessing possible products to sell, you need to take stock of your current financial situation. Are you able to start and support your business financially for about a year before it can pick up and give back some significant profit? If your financial situation is good, you will be better placed to see your small business grow.

Remember that the starting point for any business is to conduct a survey of the market, to identify gaps in the market. You would be failing if you set up a vending machine to offer the same products that an adjacent one is offering because then, you will not be capturing the attention of the consumers sufficiently.

Therefore, before you decide on the products to offer your customers, conduct a survey of the local market, visiting retail stores and public places that have vending machines. See what other vendors are offering. Are they selling gourmet foods, health foods, or the average beverage and snack? Would you want to sell something besides the food? Getting a precise answer to these and other questions you may raise will guide your decision-making, and the direction the actions you take in regard to your new business.

One more thing that sets vendors off is the unrealistic expectations they set regarding their businesses. Be realistic about the profits you expect to make, and the costs involved. Also, be sure to set aside time for servicing, restocking

and collecting your money so that you will not
incur some unnecessary labor costs.

Idea #13: Be Paid To Have an App in Your Phone

It is difficult to run your life without using an app here and another there. Our lives have become so intricately intertwined with technology that almost all that we do; we require an app to do it effectively. Unbeknownst to many, some apps pay you for using them for only a few seconds. However, you have to get the right ones to make having them worth your while.

Unfortunately, you may have found many articles talking about paying apps, but the reality is that most of these apps are not worth having at all. Some take up too much of your precious time, with little or no return, while others do not offer the compensation at all. To that end, below is a short list of some of the tested and tried apps for which you will receive some money for using.

a. UberEATS is one app that does more than give you some cash back; it allows you to make an income. UberEATS is just like the regular Uber, only that instead of giving rides to people, you do deliveries of packages, food or even flowers. Working with this app, you get to set your own schedule and earn money whenever you can.

The deliveries do not necessarily have to be made using a car, but that largely depends on the city laws. You could also use a scooter or a bike. If you are using a car, remember that you have to adhere to the laws of the road, such as having a valid driving license, and insurance for your vehicle. Uber also conducts a thorough background check, and require delivery persons to be 19 years or older.

b. Ibotta: Using the Ibotta app, you stand to gain some money when you go buying groceries. The app's system works like coupons. You only select the reimbursements that you have of items in your grocery list and then scan the receipt. You then later receive money deposited in your account, in a span of 48 hours. You could also receive the money via PayPal.

c. Inbox Dollars: This is an app that asks for your opinions and later pays you for them. You only have to answer a few survey questions about the products you use and the places you visit regularly. Membership for this app is free, and you will only be requested to submit your email address. Both Apple and Android users can access this app on their phones. For their participation, they receive gift cards, money via PayPal, and can be entered into draws to win other fantastic prizes.

d. Airbnb: This is another app that lets you earn a significant amount of income, provided you have some spare space in your house. You get to host people in your house when you are out of town, but you can still rent out your spare room or guest house. You only have to list the space you are offering, the location, and the rates on Airbnb, and persons whose needs match what you are offering will contact you. You get to set your rate, which means that you can earn a significant income from this activity all year long.

e. Stockpile: this is an investment app. It allows you to invest in fractional shares of your favorite stocks with as little as $5, going up. You are not asked to pay any monthly fees, but for every transaction, you engage in, whether a buy or a sell, you pay 99 cents. You also get to move your money from your app to the bank and vice versa, for free. Dividends from your transactions can be reinvested at no charge. This app offers an ideal custodial account for your child.

f. Letgo: this app is designed to help you get rid of unwanted stuff in your space. With the app, you can sell these items locally. So far, this app has had millions of downloads in America as people strive to declutter. You may be able to find a buyer for your old shoes, suits, furniture, car, and other unwanted stuff.

Other apps with which you could earn some money include BookScouter, Decluttr, Acorns, Wag Walking, Poshmark, Field Agent, HealthyWage, Ebates, StepBet, Swagbucks, and Shopkick.
YouTube Ads

The process of making money on YouTube is simple: you post some videos, viewers are attracted to your content, and you can then cash in on the ads placed in them. This statement makes it seem so simple and easy, but as you will find out, it is not. It is difficult to get traffic to your YouTube channel, but once this is done, you shouldn't strain as much.

Don't be worried though; the video world makes money faster than the writing world because people would rather watch videos than reading blog posts because of our attention spans. In addition, Google searches favor YouTube in their results, and tend to place them at the top of the page, without really scrutinizing the quality of the video. It only considers the tags, title, and description. This does not even remotely compare to what it takes to get your article ranking high on the Google results.

The first source of revenue that you should explore as you get into the YouTube business is the ads. The first thing to do is to become a YouTube Partner, which you can do very quickly in the Creator Studio section of your account. Just go to the Channel menu, verify your account, and enable the Monetization option.

Once you become a Partner, you need to have an AdSense account so that you can finally become part of Google's advertising network so that you can begin to have an income flow from your ad revenue reports.

When that is done, a green dollar sign will begin to appear next to your videos on the Video Manager, and this should be confirmed on whether the channel has been monetized or not. Each video should also be monetized individually. As you will see, it's easy to set this system up.

Only remember that you need to have garnered at least 10k view to be eligible for the Partner Program, but when it comes to payment, you will be paid via something called the Cost per Mileage (CPM). Typically, the CPM is 1,000 views, and for this, you will get between 1 and 3 dollars, on average. Therefore, if you receive 10,000 views on your monetized video, you should get between 10 and 30 dollars in revenue.

Seek to monetize your YouTube channel. Approach it from a business perspective, and diversify your risk with different channels, and different ways to make money from your videos. You will be glad you did, especially when the cheques begin to arrive.

Idea #14: Designing Merchandise

As a designer, you do not have to wait until your big break when you become a star to make money; you can begin to find your way to recognition as early as now. You could design a theme and sell it to Wordpress, you could come up with a t-shirt design, and you could design suits and other clothes, and even design fonts and pictures for wall hangings or to be engraved in different items. There is not an end to the range of things you can create with your mind and sell to the highest bidder.

Amazon has created room for this craft through its Merch feature that allows designers to come up with t-shirt designs, upload them to Amazon, and then get a commission for each t-shirt sold. The amount you get in royalties will depend on the price you have set for your t-shirts.

The great advantage of having Merch is that you do not need to be an excellent graphic designer to sell your designs, but this is primarily because most fast-moving designs are based on text. Therefore, using only text, you can create great merchandise that will earn you a significant income.

Designing has become especially easy with the advent of great free programs and mobile apps that make for great tools to create simple yet fascinating designs. In addition, you need very little time to bring together a design. You can spend just five hours of your time every week, and still earn quite a decent income.

Another advantage of selling merchandise is that you do not have to market it to the actual clients; you only have to upload your designs to the platform with which you have partnered. For example, if you choose Merch, you only need to upload your designs to Amazon, and you will be opened up to a world with millions of buyers. Amazon is the largest marketplace, globally. No need to worry about customer reviews with this one because your designs will not be reliant on their opinions. What looks good to one person could get a contrary review from another customer.

You will also be happy to know that most platforms will not charge any fees, with the example of the Merch platform. Amazon will take care of all shipping, printing, inventory, and customer service, and all you have to do is to upload the designs. You do not also get to pay for the uploads, and Amazon will only take a proportion of the money from the sale. Although some people go ahead and purchase paid design software, this is truly not necessary; you can do just as well with free software.

The only downside of using the Merch feature on Amazon is that you cannot just sign up and be approved immediately. There is such a long waiting list due to high demand, which makes the approval process take quite a long time, sometimes, months.

Conclusion

Thank for making it through to the end of *Passive Income Ideas*, let's hope it was informative and able to provide you with all of the tools you need to achieve your goals whatever it is that they may be. It is exciting to see just how many potential money-making opportunities we have been sleeping on. Did you know someone could pay you to take a nap at your house? Did you know your empty driveway could make you an income? It is amazing the number of opportunities that lie around that we could turn around, to increase our incomes.

Take up any opportunity to make passive money, so long as it is legal because, in truth, none of us ever has enough money. In addition, none of us is assured of tomorrow. You may be holding a good high-paying job today, and lose it tomorrow. What happens then? Having a prestigious day job is not enough. Having a good business is not enough either because an economic downturn or a natural occurrence could bring everything down. The reality is that each one of us needs multiple sources of income to stay afloat, whatever comes up.

The next step after learning various interesting ways you can earn extra income is to go ahead and try a few of them. If you love writing, start a blog. If you like designing things, go ahead and look for platforms from which to sell your merchandise. You could also start a pyramid scheme if your conscience allows it. The number of possible ventures is endless, even beyond those listed in this book. Go forth now, and grow your income sources, to ensure that your present and your future are protected.

Finally, if you found this book useful in any way, a review on Amazon is always appreciated!